Impressum / legal notice

1. Auflage / 1. Edition


Kontakt / contact:
Fernando Carrillo Castillo
Am Fackelstein 3a
56305 Puderbach, Germany

Covergestaltung / cover design:
Fernando Carrillo Castillo

Made in the USA
Monee, IL
28 October 2022

16755600R00061